The Kids' Career Library™

A Day in the Life of an
Architect

Mary Bowman-Kruhm

The Rosen Publishing Group's
PowerKids Press

Thanks to Katie Kruhm and to the architecture firm of Cooper Carry
for their help with this book.

Published in 1999 by The Rosen Publishing Group, Inc.
29 East 21st Street, New York, NY 10010

First Edition

Book Design: Erin McKenna

Photo Illustrations: All photos by Ethan Zindler.

Bowman-Kruhm, Mary.
    A day in the life of an architect / by Mary Bowman-Kruhm.
        p.   cm. — (The kids' career library)
    Includes index.
    Summary: Describes some of the aspects of an architect's work by following a project from idea through construction to completion.
    ISBN 0-8239-5297-5
    1.Architectural practice—Juvenile literature. [1. Architects. 2. Occupations.]
    I. Title. II. Series.
NA1996.B68 1998
720'.68—dc21

                                             98-9262
                                            CIP
                                            AC

Manufactured in the United States of America

Contents

Architect Katie

Every day on her way to work, Katie passes a fountain. She thinks back to the first plans that showed how the **structure** (STRUK-sher) would look. As an **architect** (AR-kih-tekt), Katie helped **design** (deh-ZYN) the plans to build the fountain. Stores, schools, zoos, pools, houses, hospitals, along with places to worship, work, shop, and eat all start with plans designed by an architect like Katie!

◀ Katie likes to look at her finished projects. They remind her of all the hard work that was done on them.

Projects, Big and Little

Architect Katie worked with many people on the fountain for about nine months. It started as plans on paper and has become a place everyone can enjoy. The fountain was a small **project** (PRAH-jekt). A big project, such as a mall, may have huge buildings, parking lots, and open spaces. That kind of project takes many years to design and build. One project that Katie worked on is the Colorado Retail Center. It took five years to build, from start to finish.

Every architecture project begins ▶ with a written plan on paper.

"We Work Together!"

Whether it's a big project or a little one, architects must first decide how a project will look when it is done. They must also decide what each person will do to help it look that way. Katie likes to work with other people. She knows that, no matter what kind of project it is, she will work with many people who have many different jobs. "Any building is a team project. No one person can do it alone," Architect Katie says.

◀ Working as part of a team helps Katie create new ideas for a project.

Playing with Ideas

For a big project, a team of architects works on the plans. Everything must be designed, such as how two walls will come together and how the doors will look. Making these plans takes a lot of thinking. The office where Katie works has toys for the architects to play with. Katie and the other architects play with these toys while they think about building plans. "Playing with toys helps me come up with good ideas," says Katie.

On some days Katie plays with the architecture toys while she eats her lunch. ▶

From Ideas to Plans

Architect Katie must turn the ideas in her head into plans that others can see. She spends a lot of time working at her computer. There she designs the details of windows, walls, and doors. She might also draw with crayons and colored markers. She may make a model to help the other architects see how the building will look when it's done. As Katie and the other architects work, they talk and share ideas.

◀ Working with colored markers helps architects like Katie show more detail in their designs.

Making a Drawing Set

At last the team of architects puts their work together. Now other people are needed to build a **drawing set** (DRAW-ing SET). This is a tiny version of what the architects have designed. It looks like a tiny building for tiny people! The drawing set helps the architects see what the finished project will look like before building begins.

A drawing set helps the team make final decisions about their project. ▶

To Work

Work moves to the **building site** (BIL-ding SYT) and more people join the team. Each person has a job to do. **Engineers** (en-jih-NEERZ) decide on the best way to build what they see on the drawing set. Then the **construction crews** (kun-STRUK-shun KROOZ) begin the work of putting up the building. They will work together using different **materials** (muh-TEER-ee-ulz) and tools until the job is finished.

◀ Katie often visits the building site to answer the builders' questions.

During Construction

Architect Katie's work doesn't stop when construction starts. During construction, Katie visits the building site. She checks that **codes** (KOHDZ) are followed. Codes are rules that tell how buildings must be built so they are safe and **comfortable** (KUMF-ter-buhl). Katie also checks to be sure the work is done the way the architects planned. If it is not, Katie meets with the engineers and construction crew to work out any problems.

Safety at a building site is always important, so Katie wears a hard hat whenever she is at a site. ▶

Solving Problems

What if a problem comes up about how to heat the building? The engineers figure out how to solve the problem. The architects work with the engineers to choose a place where the heater won't stick out or look silly. Then the construction crews put in the heater and the **ducts** (DUKTS) that are needed to carry heat to all parts of the building. "I like being an architect because every day is different, with something new to learn," says Katie.

◀ All projects at Katie's job receive careful attention and are done with care.

Pride in Her Work

Like most architects, Architect Katie is proud of what she does. She works hard to turn ideas into buildings that people can use.

"It's great to see people use and enjoy something I've designed," she says. When you walk into a building, you may not realize all of the work that goes into it. But now you can think about the work done by Katie and architects like her. What an interesting job!

Glossary

architect (AR-kih-tekt) Someone who designs buildings.

building site (BIL-ding SYT) The place where the building of a project takes place.

code (KOHD) A rule about how a building must be built.

comfortable (KUMF-ter-buhl) Feeling at ease.

construction crew (kun-STRUK-shun KROO) The people who build a project.

design (deh-ZYN) To make a plan for.

drawing set (DRAW-ing SET) The plans telling how a building is to be built; a small version of a project.

duct (DUKT) A pipe that carries heat.

engineer (en-jih-NEER) Someone trained to carry out plans for a project.

material (muh-TEER-ee-ul) What something is made of.

project (PRAH-jekt) A building on which a group of people work.

structure (STRUK-sher) Something that is built.

Index